Air Fryer Recipes

The perfect cookbook for preparing delicious meals with your Instant Vortex

Joanna Smith

© Copyright 2021 - All rights reserved.

Table of contents

BREAKFAST AND BRUNCH

1. Soufflé

Preparation Time: 5 minutes

Cooking Time: 15 minutes

Servings: 4

Ingredients:

- Six eggs
- 1/3 of cup of milk
- ½ cup of shredded mozzarella cheese
- 1 tablespoon of freshly chopped parsley
- ½ cup of chopped ham
- ½ teaspoon of garlic powder
- 1 teaspoon of salt
- 1 teaspoon of pepper

Directions:

- Grease four ramekins with a nonstick cooking spray. Preheat your air fryer to 350 degrees F.

- Using a bowl, add and mix all the ingredients properly.

- Pour the egg mixture into the greased ramekins and place it inside your air fryer.

- Cook it inside your oven for eight minutes. Then carefully remove the soufflé from your air fryer and allow it to cool off.

Nutrition: Calories 195 Fat 15g Carbs 6g Protein 9g

2. Steak and Eggs

Servings: 4

Preparation Time: 10 minutes

Cooking Time: 30 minutes

Ingredients:

- Cooking oil spray

- 4 (4-ounce) New York strip steaks

- 1 teaspoon granulated garlic, divided

- Four eggs

- 1 teaspoon salt, divided

- 1 teaspoon freshly ground black pepper, divided

- ½ teaspoon paprika

Directions:

- Insert the crisper plate into the basket and the basket into the unit. Preheat the unit by selecting air fry, setting the temperature to 360 degrees F, and setting the time to three minutes Select start to begin.

- Once the unit is preheated, spray the crisper plate with cooking oil. Place two steaks into the basket; do not oil or season them at this time.

- Select air fry, set the temperature to 360 degrees F, and set the time to nine minutes Select start.

- After five minutes, open the unit and flip the steaks. Sprinkle each with ¼ teaspoon of salt, ¼ teaspoon of granulated garlic, and ¼ teaspoon of pepper. Resume cooking until the steaks register at least 145 degrees F on a food thermometer.

- When the cooking is complete, transfer the steaks to a plate and tent with foil to keep warm. Repeat steps 2, 3, and 4 with the remaining steaks.

- Spray four ramekins with oil. Crack one egg into each ramekin. Sprinkle the eggs with the paprika and remaining ½ teaspoon each of salt and pepper. Work in batches, place two ramekins into the basket.

- Select BAKE, set the temperature to 330 degrees F, and set the time to five minutes Select start to begin. When the cooking is complete and the eggs are cooked to 160 degrees F, remove the ramekins and repeat step 7 with the remaining two ramekins.

- Serve the eggs with the steaks.

Nutrition: Calories 304 Fat 19g Carbs 2g Protein 31g

BREAD, PIZZA AND PASTA

3. Crust-less Meaty Pizza

Preparation time: 10 minutes

Cooking time: 15 minutes

Servings: 4

Ingredients:

- 1/2 cup mozzarella cheese, shredded

- Two slices sugar-free bacon, cooked and crumbled

- ¼ cup ground sausage, cooked

- Seven slices pepperoni

- 1 tbsp. parmesan cheese, grated

Directions:

- Spread the mozzarella across the bottom of a six-inch cake pan. Throw on the sausage, bacon, and pepperoni, then add a sprinkle of the parmesan cheese on top. Place the pan inside your oven.

- Cook at 400 degrees F for five minutes. The cheese is ready once brown in color and bubbly. Take care when removing the pan from the air fryer.

Nutrition: Calories: 374 Carbs: 57 g Fat: 4 g.

4. Mac and Cheese

Preparation Time: 10 minutes

Cooking Time: 30 minutes

Serve: 6

Ingredients:

- 2 1/2 cups pasta, uncooked
- 1/2 cup cream
- 2 tbsp. flour
- 1 cup vegetable broth
- 1/2 cup parmesan cheese, grated
- 1/2 cup Velveeta cheese, cut into small cubes
- Two cups Colby cheese, shredded
- 2 tbsp. butter
- 1 tsp. salt

Directions:

- Cook pasta according to the packet instructions. Drain well.

- Melt butter in a pan over medium heat. Slowly whisk in flour.

- Whisk constantly and slowly add the broth.

- Slowly pour the cream and whisk constantly.

- Slowly add Velveeta cheese, parmesan cheese, and Colby cheese and whisk until smooth.

- Add cooked pasta to the sauce and mix well to coat.

- Transfer pasta into the greased casserole dish.

- Set to bake at 350 degrees F for thirty-five minutes. After five minutes, place the casserole dish in the preheated oven.

Nutrition: Calories 410 Fat 21.8 g Carbs 34 g

5. Fitness Bread

Preparation time: 10 minutes

Cooking time: 80 minutes

Servings: 1 bread

Ingredients:

- 150 g whole wheat flour

- 150 g whole meal rye flour

- tbsp. agave syrup, alternatively also maple syrup

- 25 g yeast

- tsp. salt

- tbsp. flaxseed oil

- 40 g chopped walnuts

- 35 g chopped pumpkin seeds

- 50 g dried fruit of your choice cut into pieces (dates, raisins, etc.) Water

Directions:

- Sieve wheat and rye flour and add salt. Dissolve the yeast in lukewarm water and mix in agave syrup. Add the flour and oil and knead everything into a soft dough. Then cover a clean kitchen towel with the dough and let it rest in a warm position for 30 minutes.

- In the meantime, stir the chopped nuts and kernels with the dried fruit cut into pieces and, after the resting time, knead well into the dough.

- Place the dough in the baking pan of the air fryer and cover it for another fifteen minutes. Then program the oven to 390 degrees F and bake the loaf for five minutes. Then reduce the temperature to 350 degrees F and bake for another fifty-five minutes. Brush the bread with a little water now and then to create a shiny crust.

Nutrition: Calories: 927 Fat: 31.24 g Carbs: 147.53 g

SNACKS AND APPETIZERS

6. Cheesy Garlic Dip

Preparation Time: 10 Minutes

Cooking Time: 20 minutes

Servings: 12

Ingredients:

- 4 garlic cloves, minced

- 5 oz Asiago cheese, shredded

- 1 cup mozzarella cheese, shredded

- 8 oz cream cheese, softened 1 cup sour cream

Directions:

- Add all ingredients into the mixing bowl and mix until well combined.

- Pour mixture into the baking dish.

- Set to bake at 350 degrees F for 25 minutes. After 5 minutes place the baking dish in the preheated oven.

Nutrition: Calories 157 Fat 14.4 g Carbs 1.7 g

7. Cheese Brussels Sprouts

Preparation Time: 10 Minutes

Cooking Time: 12 minutes

Servings: 4

Ingredients:

- 1 lb Brussels sprouts, cut stems and halved

- 1/4 cup parmesan cheese, grated

- 1 tablespoon olive oil

- 1/4 teaspoon paprika

- 1/4 teaspoon chili powder

- 1/2 teaspoon garlic powder

- Salt and Pepper

Directions:

- Stir Brussels sprouts with remaining ingredients except for cheese and place in air fryer basket then place air fryer basket in baking pan.

- Place a baking pan on the oven rack. Set to air fry at 350 degrees F for 12 minutes.

- Top with parmesan cheese.

Nutrition: Calories 100 Fat 5.2 g Carbs 11 g

8. Cheese Onion Dip

Preparation Time: 10 Minutes

Cooking Time: 40 minutes

Servings: 8

Ingredients:

- 1 1/2 onions, chopped
- 1/2 teaspoon garlic powder
- 1 1/2 cup Swiss cheese, shredded
- 1 cup mozzarella cheese, shredded
- 1 cup cheddar cheese, shredded
- 1 1/2 cup mayonnaise
- Salt and Pepper

Directions:

- Add all ingredients into the mixing bowl and mix until well combined.
- Pour mixture into the prepared baking dish.

- Set to bake at 350 degrees F for 45 minutes. After 5 minutes place the baking dish in the preheated oven.

Nutrition: Calories 325 Fat 25.7 g Carbs 14 g

9. Cheese Spinach Dip

Preparation Time: 10 Minutes

Cooking Time: 20 minutes

Servings: 12

Ingredients:

- 3 oz frozen spinach, defrosted & chopped

- 1 cup sour cream

- 2 cups cheddar cheese, shredded

- 8 oz cream cheese

- 1 teaspoon garlic salt

Directions:

- Add all ingredients into the mixing bowl and mix well.

- Transfer mixture into the baking dish.

- Set to bake at 350 degrees F for 25 minutes. After 5 minutes place the baking dish in the preheated oven.

Nutrition: Calories 185 Fat 16.9 g Carbs 2 g

MAINS

10. urried Chicken, Chickpeas and Raita Salad

Preparation Time: 10 minutes

Cooking time: 30 minutes

Servings: 5

Ingredients:

- 1 cup red grapes halved

- 3-4 cups rotisserie chicken, meat coarsely shredded

- 2 tbsp cilantro

- 1 cup plain yogurt

- Two medium tomatoes, chopped

- 1 tsp ground cumin

- 1 tbsp minced peeled ginger

- 1 tbsp minced garlic

- One medium onion, chopped

- 1 tbsp curry powder

- 2 tbsp vegetable oil

Chickpeas Ingredients:

- ¼ tsp. cayenne

- 1/2 tsp. turmeric

- 1 tsp ground cumin

- one 19-oz can chickpeas, rinsed, drained, and patted dry

- 1 tbsp vegetable oil

Topping and Raita Ingredients:

- 1/2 cup sliced and toasted almonds

- 2 tbsp chopped mint

- 1 cup plain yogurt

- 2 cups cucumber, peeled, cored, and chopped

Directions:

- To make the chicken salad, place a medium nonstick saucepan and heat oil on a medium-low fire.

- Sauté ginger, garlic, and onion for 5 minutes or until softened while stirring occasionally.

- Add 1 1/2 tsp.: salt, cumin, and curry. Sauté for two minutes.

- Increase fire to medium-high and add tomatoes. Stirring frequently, cook for 5 minutes.

- Pour sauce into a bowl, mix in chicken, cilantro, and yogurt. Stir to combine and let it stand to cool to room temperature.

- To make the chickpeas, on a nonstick fry pan, heat oil for 3 minutes.

- Add chickpeas and cook for a minute while stirring frequently.

- Add ¼ tsp.: salt, cayenne, turmeric, and cumin. Stir to mix well and cook for two minutes or until sauce is dried.

- Transfer to a bowl and let it cool to room temperature.

- To make the raita, mix 1/2 tsp.: salt, mint, cucumber, and yogurt. Stir thoroughly to combine and dissolve the salt.

- In four 16-oz lidded jars or bowls, to assemble, layer the following: curried chicken, raita, chickpeas, and garnish with almonds.

- You can make this recipe one day ahead and refrigerate for 6 hours before serving.

Nutrition: Calories 403, Fat 16g, Carbs 42g

11.   Curried Coconut Chicken

Preparation Time: 10 minutes

Cooking time: 40 minutes

Servings: 6

Ingredients:

- 4 large tomatoes, sliced

- 1 can make coconut milk (14-oz)

- 6 cloves garlic, crushed then minced

- 1 whole onion, sliced thinly

- 1 tbsp curry

- 1 tbsp. turmeric

- 1 tsp. cinnamon

- 1 tsp. clove powder

- 1 tsp. fenugreek

- 1-inch long ginger around thumb-sized, peeled

- 2 bay leaves

- 2 lbs. boneless and skinless chicken breasts cut into 1-inch cubes

- 2 cups of water

- ¼ of the red bell pepper cut into 1-inch thick strips

- 1/2 tsp. salt

- 1 tsp. pepper

- 2 tbsp olive oil

Directions:

- In a heavy-bottomed pot, heat oil on the medium-high fire.

- Sauté garlic and ginger until garlic is starting to brown, around 1 to 2 minutes.

- Add curry, turmeric, cinnamon, clove, bay leaf, and fenugreek. Sauté until fragrant, around 3 to 5 minutes.

- Add tomatoes and onions. Sauté for 5 to ten minutes or until tomatoes are wilted, and onions are soft and translucent. If needed, add ¼ cup of water.

- Add chicken breasts and sauté for 5 minutes—season with pepper and salt.

- Add remaining water; bring to a boil, then slow fire to medium. While covered, continue cooking chicken for at least 15 minutes.

- Add bell pepper and coconut milk. Cook until heated through.

- Turn off fire and serve best with brown rice.

Nutrition: Calories 225, Fat 8g, Carbs 12g

12.   Eggplant Fries

Preparation time: 10 minutes

Cooking time: 5 minutes

Servings: 4

Ingredients:

- 1 eggplant, peeled and sliced
- 1 flax-egg
- ½ cup cashew cheese
- 2 tbsp. almond milk
- 2 cups almond meal
- Salt and Black pepper
- Cooking spray

Directions:

- Take a bowl and add flax egg, salt, and pepper to it
- Whisk it well
- Take another bowl, mix cheese and panko, then stir

- Dip eggplant fries in the flax egg mixture, coat in panko mix

- Grease the Air Fryer basket using vegan cooking spray

- Place the eggplant fries in it

- Cook for 5 minutes at 400 degrees

Nutrition: Calories: 162 Fat: 5g Carbs: 7g Protein: 6g

13. Vegan Taquito

Preparation time: 15 minutes

Cooking time: 15 minutes

Servings: 4

Ingredients:

- 8 corn tortillas

- 1 (15 ounces) can vegan refried beans

- 1 cup shredded vegan cheese

- Guacamole

- Cashew cheese

- Vegan sour cream

- Fresh salsa

- Cooking oil spray

Directions:

- Preheat your Air Fryer to 392 degrees F

- Warm your tortilla and run them underwater for a second, transfer to Air Fryer cooking basket and cook for 1 minute

- Remove to the flat surface and place equal amounts of beans at the center of each tortilla, top with vegan cheese

- Roll tortilla sides up over filling, place seam side down in Air Fryer

- Spray oil on top and cook for 7 minutes until golden brown

Nutrition: Calories: 420 Fat: 5g Carbs: 80g

14.   Turkey and Broccoli Stew

Preparation Time: 10 minutes

Cooking Time: 30 minutes

Serving: 4

Ingredients:

- 1 turkey breast, skinless; boneless, and cubed
- 1 broccoli head, florets separated
- 1 cup tomato sauce
- 1 tbsp. Parsley, chopped.
- Salt and pepper
- 1 tbsp. olive oil

Directions:

- In a baking dish that fits your air fryer, mix the turkey with the rest of the ingredients except the parsley, toss, introduce the plate in the fryer, bake at 380°F for 25 minutes
- Divide into bowls and sprinkle the parsley on top.

Nutrition: Calories: 250; Fat: 11g; Carbs: 6g

15. Turkey and Mushroom Stew

Preparation Time: 10 minutes

Cooking Time: 30 minutes

Serving: 4

Ingredients:

- 1 turkey breast, skinless, boneless; cubed and browned

- 1/2 lb. brown mushrooms; sliced

- ¼ cup tomato sauce

- 1 tbsp. Parsley, chopped.

- Salt and pepper

Directions:

- In a pan that fits your air fryer, mix the turkey with the mushrooms, salt, pepper, and tomato sauce toss, introduce to the fryer and cook at 350°F for 25 minutes

- Divide into bowls and serve with parsley sprinkled on top.

Nutrition: Calories: 220; Fat: 12g; Carbs: 5g

16.   Turkey and Quinoa Stuffed Peppers

Preparation Time: 15 minutes

Cooking time: 35 minutes

Servings: 6

Ingredients:

- 3 large red bell peppers

- 2 tsp chopped fresh rosemary

- 2 tbsp chopped fresh parsley

- 3 tbsp chopped pecans, toasted

- 1/2 cup chicken stock

- 1/2 lb. fully cooked smoked turkey sausage, diced

- 2 cups of water

- 2 tbsp. extra virgin olive oil

- 1 cup uncooked quinoa 1/2 tsp. salt

Directions:

- On high fire, place a large saucepan and add salt, water, and quinoa. Bring to a boil.

- Once boiling, reduce fire to a simmer, cover, and cook until all water is absorbed, around 15 minutes.

- Uncover quinoa, turn off the fire, and let it stand for another 5 minutes.

- Add rosemary, parsley, pecans, olive oil, chicken stock, and turkey sausage into quinoa pan. Mix well.

- Slice peppers lengthwise in half and discards membranes and seeds. In another boiling pot of water, add peppers, boil for 5 minutes, drain and discard water.

- Grease a 13 x 9 baking dish and preheat oven to 3500F.

- Place boiled bell pepper onto a prepared baking dish, evenly fill with the quinoa mixture, and pop into the oven.

- Bake for 15 minutes.

Nutrition: Calories 253, Fat 13g, Carbs 21g, Protein 14g

17. Chicken and Asparagus

Preparation Time: 25 minutes

Cooking Time: 20 minutes

Serving: 4

Ingredients:

- Four chicken breasts, skinless; boneless and halved
- One bunch asparagus; trimmed and halved
- 1 tbsp. Sweet paprika
- Salt and pepper
- 1 tbsp. Olive oil

Directions:

- Take a bowl and mix all the ingredients, toss, put them in your air fryer's basket and cook at 390°f for 20 minutes

Nutrition: Calories: 230; Fat: 11g; Carbs: 5g; Protein: 12g

POULTRY

18. Chicken Pram

Preparation Time: 10 minutes

Cooking time: 35 minutes

Servings: 4

Ingredients:

- 4 chicken breast halves, skinless & boneless
- 1/2 cup flour
- 2 eggs
- 2/3 cup panko breadcrumbs
- 2/3 cup Italian seasoned breadcrumbs
- 1/3 + ¼ cup parmesan cheese, divided

44

- 2 tbsp. fresh parsley, chopped

- Nonstick cooking spray

- 24 oz. marinara sauce

- 1 cup mozzarella cheese, grated

- 1/2 tsp. salt

- ¼ tsp. pepper

Directions:

- Place the baking pan in position 2 of the oven. Lightly spray the fryer basket with cooking spray.

- Place flour in a shallow dish.

- In a separate shallow dish, beat the eggs.

- In a third shallow dish, combine both breadcrumbs, 1/3 cup parmesan cheese, two tablespoons parsley, salt, and pepper.

- Place chicken between two sheets of plastic wrap and pound to 1/2-inch thick.

- Dip chicken first in flour, then eggs, and breadcrumb mixture to coat. Place in the basket and then put the basket on the baking pan.

- Set oven to air fry on 375°F for 10 minutes. Turn chicken over halfway through cooking time.

- Remove chicken and baking pan from the oven. Set range to bake on 425°F for 30 minutes.

- Pour 1 1/2 cups marinara in the bottom of an 8x11-inch baking dish. Place chicken over the sauce and add another two tablespoons marinara to tops of chicken. Top the chicken with mozzarella and parmesan cheese once oven preheats for 5 minutes, place the dish in the oven and bake 20-25 minutes until bubbly and cheese is golden brown. Nutrition:

Nutrition: Calories: 529 kcal/Cal Fat: 13 g Carbs: 52 g Protein: 51 g

19. Chicken Stir-Fry

Preparation Time: 10 minutes

Cooking Time: 20 minutes

Servings: 2

Ingredients:

- 1 (6-oz.) chicken breast; cut into 1-inch cubes

- 1/2 medium red bell pepper; seeded and chopped

- 1/2 medium zucchini; chopped

- ¼ medium red onion; peeled and sliced

- 1/2 tsp. Garlic powder

- 1 tsp. Dried oregano

- ¼ tsp. dried thyme

- 1 tbsp. Coconut oil

Directions:

- Place all ingredients into a large mixing bowl and toss until the coconut oil coats the meat and vegetables. Pour the contents of the bowl into the air fryer basket

- Adjust the temperature to 375°F and set the timer for 15 minutes. Shake the fryer basket halfway through the cooking time to redistribute the food.

Nutrition: Calories: 186 kcal/Cal Protein: 20.4 g Fat: 8.0 g Carbs: 5.6 g

20. Chicken with Oregano-Orange Chimichurri

Preparation Time: 5 minutes

Cooking Time: 12 minutes

Servings: 4

Ingredients:

- 700g chicken breast, cut into 4 pieces

- 1 teaspoon finely grated orange zest

- 1 teaspoon dried oregano

- One small garlic clove, grated

- 2 teaspoon vinegar (red wine, cider, or white wine)

- 1 tablespoon fresh orange juice

- 1/2 cup chopped fresh flat-leaf parsley leaves

- Sea salt and pepper

- 1/4 cup and 2 teaspoons extra virgin olive oil

- 4 cups arugula

- Two bulbs fennel, shaved

- 2 tablespoons whole-grain mustard

Directions:

- Make chimichurri: In a medium bowl, combine orange zest, oregano, and garlic. Mix in vinegar, orange juice, and parsley and then slowly whisk in ¼ cup of olive oil until emulsified. Season with sea salt and pepper.

- Sprinkle the chicken with salt and pepper and set your air fryer toast oven to 350 degrees F.

- Brush the chicken steaks with the remaining olive oil and cook for about 6 minutes per side or until evenly browned. Take out from the fryer and let rest for at least 10 minutes.

- Toss the cooked chicken, greens, and fennel with mustard in a medium bowl; season with salt and pepper.

- Serve steak with chimichurri and salad.

Nutrition: Calories: 312 kcal Carbs: 12.8 g Fat: 33.6 g Protein: 29 g

21.   Chimichurri Turkey

Preparation Time: 20 minutes

Cooking Time: 50 minutes

Servings: 4

Ingredients:

- 1 lb. Turkey breast

- 1/2 cup chimichurri sauce

- 1/2 cup butter

- ¼ cup parmesan cheese, grated

- ¼ tsp. garlic powder

Directions:

- Massage the chimichurri sauce over turkey breast, refrigerate in an airtight container for at least a half-hour.

- Meanwhile, prepare the herbed butter. Mix the butter, parmesan, and garlic powder, using a hand mixer if you like (this will make it extra creamy)

- Preheat your fryer at 350°F and place a wire rack inside. Remove the turkey from the refrigerator and let it to return to room temperature for about 20 minutes while the fryer warms.

- Place the turkey in the fryer and allow it to cool for 20 minutes. Flip and cook on the other side for another 20 minutes.

- Take care when removing the turkey from the fryer. Place it on a serving dish with the herbed butter.

22. Collard Wraps with Satay Dipping Sauce

Preparation Time: 10 minutes

Cooking Time: 16 minutes

Servings: 6

Ingredients:

- Wraps 4 large collard leaves, stems removed

- Six (200g) grilled chicken breasts, diced

- One medium avocado, sliced

- 1/2 cucumber, thinly sliced

- One cup diced mango

- Six large strawberries, thinly sliced

- 24 mint leaves

- Dipping Sauce

- 2 tablespoons almond butter

- 2 tablespoons coconut cream

- 1 bird eye chili, finely chopped

- 2 tablespoons unsweetened applesauce

- ¼ cup fresh lime juice

- 1 teaspoon sesame oil

- 1 tablespoon apple cider vinegar

- 1 tablespoon tahini

- 1 clove garlic, crushed

- 1 tablespoon grated fresh ginger

- 1/8 teaspoon of sea salt

Directions:

For the chicken breasts:

- Start by setting your air fryer to 350 degrees F. Lightly coat the air fryer's basket with oil.

- Season the briskets with salt and pepper and place on the prepared basket and fry for 8 minutes on each side.

- Once done, remove from the air fryer oven and place on a platter to cool slightly then dice.

For the wraps:

- Divide the vegetables and diced chicken breasts equally between the four large collard leaves; fold bottom edges over the filling. Then, both sides and roll very tightly to the end of the leaves; secure with toothpicks and cut each in half.

Make the sauce:

- Combine all the sauce ingredients in a blender and blend until very smooth. Divide among bowls and serve with the wraps.

Nutrition: Calories: 389 kcal, Carbs: 11.7 g, Fat: 38.2 g, Protein: 26 g.

23. Creamy Chicken Wings

Preparation Time: 5 minutes

Cooking Time: 30 minutes

Servings: 4

Ingredients:

- 2 lb. chicken wings

- ¼ cup parmesan, grated

- 1/2 cup heavy cream

- Three garlic cloves; minced

- 3 tbsp. Butter; melted

- 1/2 tsp. Oregano; dried

- 1/2 tsp. basil; dried

- Salt and black pepper to taste.

Directions:

- In a dish suitable for your air fryer, mix the chicken wings with all the ingredients except the parmesan cheese and toss.

- Place the dish in your air fryer and cook at 380°F for 30 minutes. Sprinkle on the cheese, set the mixture aside for 10 minutes, divide between plates.

Nutrition: Calories: 270 kcal/Cal Fat: 12 g Carbs: 6 g Protein: 17 g

RED MEAT

24. Roast Beef with Butter, Garlic and Thyme

Servings: 12

Preparation Time: 10 Minutes

Cooking Time: 120 minutes

Ingredients:

- 1 ½ tablespoon garlic

- One cup beef stock

- 1 teaspoon thyme leaves, chopped

- 3 tablespoons butter

- 3-pound eye of round roast

- 6 tablespoons extra-virgin olive oil

- 1 teaspoon pepper

- 1 teaspoon salt

Directions:

1) Place all ingredients in a Ziploc bag and let marinate in the refrigerator for 60 minutes.

2reheat the oven for five minutes.

3) Transfer all ingredients to a baking dish that fits in the air fryer.

4) Place in the air fryer and cook for 60 minutes at 400 degrees F.

5) Baste the beef with sauce every thirty minutes.

Nutrition: Calories: 273; Carbs: 0.8g; Protein: 34.2g; Fat: 14.7g

SEAFOOD

25.   Glazed Tuna and Fruit Kebabs

Preparation: 15 min Cooking 10 minutes Servings: 4

Ingredients:

Kebabs:

- 1-pound tuna steaks, cut into 1-inch cubes
- 1/2 cup canned pineapple chunks, drained, juice reserved 1/2 cup large red grapes

Marinade:

- 1 tablespoon honey
- 2 teaspoons grated fresh ginger
- 1 teaspoon olive oil

- Pinch cayenne pepper

Directions:

- Make the kebabs: Thread, pineapple chunks, alternating tuna cubes, and red grapes, onto the metal skewers.

- Make the marinade: Whisk the honey, ginger, olive oil, and cayenne pepper in a small bowl. Brush the marinade generously over the kebabs and allow them to sit for ten minutes.

- When ready, transfer the kebabs to the air fry basket.

- Select Air Fry, set the temperature to 370 degrees F, and set time to ten minutes.

- After five minutes, remove and flip the kebabs and brush with the remaining marinade. Return the basket to the oven and continue cooking for an additional five minutes.

- Remove, and discard any remaining marinade. Nutrition:

Nutrition: Calories: 319 Carbs: 0g Fat: 0g Protein: 0g

26. Golden Beer-Battered Cod

Preparation Time: 5minutes

Cooking time: 15 minutes

Servings: 4

Ingredients:

- 2 eggs
- 1 cup malty beer
- 1/2 cup cornstarch
- 1 teaspoon garlic powder
- 1 cup all-purpose flour
- Salt and pepper
- 4 (4-ounce / 113-g) cod fillets
- Cooking spray

Directions:

- In a bowl, beat together the eggs with the beer. In another bowl, thoroughly combine the flour and cornstarch. Sprinkle with the garlic powder, pepper and salt.

- Dredge each cod fillet in the flour mixture, then in the egg mixture. Dip each piece of fish in the flour mixture a second time.

- Spritz the air fry basket with cooking spray. Arrange the cod fillets in the basket in a single layer.

- Select Air Fry, set temperature to 400 degrees F, and set time to fifteen minutes. Select Start to begin preheating.

- Once preheated, place the basket on the air fry position. Flip the fillets halfway through the cooking time.

- When cooking is complete, the cod should reach an internal temperature of 145 degrees F on a meat thermometer, and the outside should be crispy. Let the fish cool for five minutes.

27. Greek Pesto Salmon

Preparation Time: 10 minutes

Cooking Time: 30 minutes

Servings: 6

Ingredients:

- Four salmon fillets

- 1/2 cup pesto

- One onion, chopped

- 2 cups grape tomatoes, halved

- 1/2 cup feta cheese, crumbled

Directions:

- Line the Baking Pan with foil and set aside.

- Place salmon fillet in baking pan and top with tomatoes, pesto, onion, and cheese.

- Set to Bake at 350 degrees F for twenty minutes.

Nutrition: Calories 447 Fat 28 g Carbs 8 g Protein 41 g

VEGETABLES

28.   Cheesy Spinach

Preparation Time: 10 Minutes

Cooking Time: 15 minutes

Servings: 4

Ingredients:

- 1 (10-ounce) package frozen spinach, thawed

- ½ cup onion, chopped

- Four ounces cream cheese, chopped

- ¼ cup Parmesan cheese, shredded

- Two teaspoons garlic, minced

- ½ teaspoon ground nutmeg

- Salt and pepper

Directions:

- In a bowl, mix well spinach, garlic, cream cheese, onion, nutmeg, salt, and pepper.

- Place spinach mixture into a baking pan.

- Preheat the Air Fryer Oven and arrange the baking pan in the basket.

- Select "Air Fry" mode and set the temperature to 350° F for ten minutes.

Nutrition: Calories: 194 Cal Fat: 15.5 g Carbs: 7.3 g Protein: 8.4 g

SOUPS

29. Vegetable and Beef Soup

Preparation Time: 35 minutes

Cooking Time: 30 minutes

Servings: 4

Ingredients:

- Two slices bacon, chopped

- 1 lb. lean ground beef

- One carrot, chopped

- Two cloves garlic, finely chopped

- One small onion, chopped

- One celery stalk, chopped

- One bay leaf; 1 teaspoon. Dried basil

- 1 cup canned tomatoes, diced and drained

- 4 cups beef broth

- ½ cup canned chickpeas

- ½ cup vermicelli

Directions:

1. In a large soup pot, cook bacon and ground beef until well done, breaking up the meat as it cooks. Drain off the fat and add in onion, garlic, carrot, and celery.

2. Cook for 3-4 minutes until fragrant. Stir in the bay leaf, basil, tomatoes, and beef broth. Bring to a boil, then reduce heat and simmer for about 20 minutes.

3. Add the chickpeas and vermicelli. Cook, uncovered, for about 5 minutes more and serves.

DESSERTS

30. Angel Cake

Preparation Time: 5 minutes

Cooking Time: 30 minutes

Serving: 4

Ingredients:

- ¼ cup butter, melted
- 1 cup powdered erythritol
- 1 teaspoon strawberry extract
- 12 egg whites
- 2teaspoons cream of tartar
- A pinch of salt

Directions:

- Preheat the air fryer for 5 minutes.

- Mix the egg whites and cream of tartar.

- Use a hand mixer and whisk until white and fluffy.

- Add the rest of the ingredients except for the butter and whisk for another minute.

- Pour into a baking dish.

- Place in the air fryer basket and cook for 30 minutes at 400°F or if a toothpick inserted in the middle comes out clean.

- Drizzle with melted butter once cooled.

Nutrition: Calories: 65; Fat: 5g; Protein: 3.1g; Fiber: 1g

FRUITS

31. Vegan Apple Cupcakes

Preparation time: 10 minutes

Cooking time: 20 minutes

Servings: 4/5

Ingredients:

- Four tbsp. vegetable oil

- Three tbsp. Flax meal combined with three tbsp. water

- ½ cup pure applesauce

- Two tsp. cinnamon powder

- One tsp. vanilla extract

- One apple, cored and chopped

- Four tsp. maple syrup

- ¾ cup whole wheat flour

- ½ tsp. baking powder

Directions:

- Heat a pan put the vegetable oil over medium heat, add flax meal, applesauce, vanilla, maple syrup, stir, take off the heat and cool down.

- Add flour, cinnamon, baking powder and apples, whisk, pour into a cupcake pan, introduce in your air fryer at 350 degrees F and bake for 20 minutes.

Nutrition: Calories 200 Fat 3g Carbs 5g Protein 4g

DIABETIC RECIPES

32.   Easy Air Fryer Zucchini Chips

(Prep Time: 10 minutes| Cook Time: 12 minutes| Servings: 2)

Ingredients

- Parmesan Cheese: 3 Tbsp.

- Garlic Powder: 1/4 tsp

- Zucchini: 1 Cup (thin slices)

- Corn Starch: 1/4 Cup

- Onion Powder: 1/4 tsp

- Salt: 1/4 tsp

- Whole wheat Bread Crumbs: 1/2 Cup

Instructions

- Let the Air Fryer preheat to 390 F. cut the zucchini into thin slices, like chips.

- In a food processor bowl, mix garlic powder, kosher salt, whole wheat bread crumbs, parmesan cheese, and onion powder.

- Blend into finer pieces.

- In three separate bowls, add corn starch in one, egg mix in another bowl, and whole wheat breadcrumb mixture in the other bowl.

- Coat zucchini chips into corn starch mix, in egg mix, then coat in whole wheat bread crumbs.

- Spray the air fryer basket with olive oil. Add breaded zucchini chips in a single layer in the air fryer and spray with olive oil.

- Air fry for six minutes at preheated temperature. Cook for another four minutes after turning or until zucchini chips are golden brown.

- Serve with any dipping sauce.

Nutritional value: Per Serving: 219 calories| total fat 26.9g

|carbohydrates 11.2g |protein 14.1g

33. Air Fryer Avocado Fries

(Prep Time: 10 minutes| Cook Time: 10 minutes| Servings: 2)

Ingredients

- One avocado

- One egg

- Whole wheat bread crumbs: 1/2 cup

- Salt: 1/2 teaspoon

Instructions

- Avocado should be firm and firm. Cut into wedges.

- In a bowl, beat egg with salt. In another bowl, add the crumbs.

- Coat wedges in egg, then in crumbs.

- Air fry them at 400F for 8-10 minutes. Toss halfway through.

- Serve hot.

Nutritional value: per serving: Calories: 251kcal | Carbohydrates: 19g | Protein: 6g | Fat: 17g |

Diabetic Turkey Recipes

34. Turkey Breast with Mustard Maple Glaze

(Prep Time: 10 minutes| Cook Time:55 minutes| Servings: 6)

Ingredients

- Whole turkey breast: 5 pounds

- Olive oil: 2 tsp.Maple syrup: 1/4 cup

- Dried sage: half tsp.

- Smoked paprika: half tsp.

- Dried thyme: one tsp.

- Salt: one tsp.

- Freshly ground black pepper: half tsp.

- Dijon mustard: 2 tbsp.

Instructions

- Let the air fryer preheat to 350 F

- Rub the olive oil all over the turkey breast

- In a bowl, mix salt, sage, pepper, thyme, and paprika. Mix well and coat turkey in this spice rub.

- Place the turkey in an air fryer, cook for 25 minutes at 350°F. Flip the turkey over and cook for another 12 minutes. Flip again and cook for another ten minutes. With an instant-read thermometer, the internal temperature should reach 165°F.

- In the meantime, in a saucepan, mix mustard, maple syrup, and with one tsp. of butter.

- Brush this glaze all over the turkey when cooked.

- Cook again for five minutes. Slice and Serve with fresh salad.

Nutritional value: per serving: Cal 379 | Fat: 23 g| Carbs: 21g | Protein: 52g

Diabetic Fish & Seafood Recipes

35. Grilled Salmon with Lemon

(Prep Time: 10 minutes| Cook Time:20 minutes| Servings: 4)

Ingredients

- Olive oil: 2 tablespoons

- Two Salmon fillets

- Lemon juice

- Water: 1/3 cup

- Gluten-free light soy sauce: 1/3 cup

- Honey: 1/3 cup

- Scallion slices

- Cherry tomato

- Freshly ground black pepper, garlic powder, kosher salt to taste

Instructions

- Season salmon with pepper and salt

- In a bowl, mix honey, soy sauce, lemon juice, water, oil. Add salmon in this marinade and let it rest for least two hours.

- Let the air fryer preheat at 180°C

- Place fish in the air fryer and cook for 8 minutes.

- Move to a dish and top with scallion slices.

Nutritional value: per serving: Cal 211| fat 9g |protein 15g| carbs 4.9g

36.   Air-Fried Fish Nuggets

(Prep Time: 15 minutes| Cook Time:10 minutes| Servings: 4)

Ingredients

- Fish fillets in cubes: 2 cups(skinless)

- 1 egg, beaten

- Flour: 5 tablespoons

- Water: 5 tablespoons

- Kosher salt and pepper to taste

- Breadcrumbs mix

- Smoked paprika: 1 tablespoon

- Whole wheat breadcrumbs: ¼ cup

- Garlic powder: 1 tablespoon

Instructions

- Season the fish cubes with kosher salt and pepper.

- In a bowl, add flour and gradually add water, mixing as you add.

- Then mix in the egg. And keep mixing but do not over mix.

- Coat the cubes in batter, then in the breadcrumb mix. Coat well

- Place the cubes in a baking tray and spray with oil.

- Let the air fryer preheat to 200 C.

- Place cubes in the air fryer and cook for 12 minutes or until well cooked and golden brown.

- Serve with salad greens.

Nutritional value: per serving: Cal 184.2|Protein: 19g| Total Fat: 3.3 g| Net Carb: 10g

Diabetic Pork Recipes

37. Air Fryer Pork Chop & Broccoli

(Prep Time: 20 minutes| Cook Time:20 minutes| Servings: 2)

Ingredients

- Broccoli florets: 2 cups

- Bone-in pork chop: 2 pieces

- Paprika: half tsp.

- Avocado oil: 2 tbsp.

- Garlic powder: half tsp.

- Onion powder: half tsp.

- Two cloves of crushed garlic

- Salt: 1 teaspoon divided

Instructions

- Let the air fryer preheat to 350 degrees. Spray the basket with cooking oil

- Add one tbsp. Oil, onion powder, half tsp. of salt, garlic powder, and paprika in a bowl mix well, rub this spice mix to the pork chop's sides

- Add pork chops to air fryer basket and let it cook for five minutes

- In the meantime, add one tsp. oil, garlic, half tsp of salt, and broccoli to a bowl and coat well

- Flip the pork chop and add the broccoli, let it cook for five more minutes.

- Take out from the air fryer and serve.

Nutritional value: per serving: Calories 483|Total Fat 20g|Carbohydrates 12g|protein 23 g

Diabetic Beef Recipes

38. Air Fryer Hamburgers

(Prep Time: 5 minutes| Cook Time:13 minutes| Servings: 4)

Ingredients

- Buns:4

- Lean ground beef chuck: 4 cups

- Salt to taste

- Slices of any cheese: 4 slices

- Black Pepper, to taste

Instructions

- Let the air fryer preheat to 350 F.

- In a bowl, add lean ground beef, pepper, and salt. Mix well and form patties.

- Put them in the air fryer in one layer only, cook for 6 minutes, flip them halfway through. One minute before you take out the patties, add cheese on top.

- When cheese is melted, take out from the air fryer.

- Add ketchup, any dressing to your buns, add tomatoes and lettuce and patties.

- Serve hot.

Nutritional value: per serving: Calories: 520kcal | Carbohydrates: 22g | Protein: 31g | Fat: 34g |

Diabetic Chicken Recipes

39. Herb-Marinated Chicken Thighs

(Prep Time: 30 minutes| Cook Time:10 minutes| Servings: 4)

Ingredients

- Chicken thighs: 8 skin-on, bone-in,

- Lemon juice: 2 Tablespoon

- Onion powder: half teaspoon

- Garlic powder: 2 teaspoon

- Spike Seasoning: 1 teaspoon.

- Olive oil: 1/4 cup

- Dried basil: 1 teaspoon

- Dried oregano: half teaspoon.

- Black Pepper: 1/4 tsp.

Instructions

- In a bowl, add dried oregano, olive oil, lemon juice, dried sage, garlic powder, Spike Seasoning, onion powder, dried basil, black pepper.

- In a ziploc bag, add the spice blend and the chicken and mix well.

- Marinate the chicken in the refrigerator for at least six hours or more.

- Preheat the air fryer to 360F.

- Put the chicken in the air fryer basket, cook for six-eight minutes, flip the chicken, and cook for six minutes more.

- Until the internal chicken temperature reaches 165F.

- Take out from the air fryer and serve with microgreens.

Nutritional value: per serving: Cal 100|Fat: 9g| Carbs 1g|Protein 4g

Diabetic Desserts Recipes

40. Air Fryer Blueberry Muffins Recipe

(Prep Time: 10 minutes| Cook Time: 12-14 minutes| Servings:

8)

Ingredients

- Half cup of sugar alternative

- One and 1/3 cup of flour 1/3 cup of oil

- Two teaspoons of baking powder

- 1/4 teaspoon of salt

- One egg Half cup of milk

- Eight muffin cups (foil) with paper liners

- Or silicone baking cups

- 2/3 cup of frozen and thawed blueberries, or fresh

Instructions

- Let the air fryer preheat to 330 F.

- In a large bowl, sift together baking powder, salt, sugar, and flour. Mix well

- In another bowl, add milk, oil, and egg mix it well.

- To the dry ingredients to the egg mix, mix until combined but do not over mix

- Add the blueberries carefully. Pour the mixture into muffin paper cups or muffin baking tray

- Put four muffin cups in the air fryer basket or add more if your basket's size is big.

- Cook for 12-14 minutes, at 330 F, or until when touch lightly the tops, it should spring back.

- Cook the remaining muffins accordingly.

- Take out from the air fryer and let them cool before serving.

Nutritional value: per serving: Cal 213|fat 10 g| Carbs 13.2 g| protein 9.7 g

30-Day Meal Plan

This meal is designed to help you achieve the best health possible. Hope you enjoy these delicious recipes that will keep your belly full and glucose level under control for days to come.

Week 1

Monday (Day 1)

Breakfast: Bell Peppers Frittata

Lunch: Lemon Rosemary Chicken

Snack: Air-Fryer Kale Chips with dipping

Dinner: Air Fryer Pork Taquitos

Tuesday (Day 2)

Breakfast: Air Fryer Crisp Egg Cups

Lunch: Air-Fried Rosemary Garlic Grilled Prawns

Snack: Air Fryer Buffalo Cauliflower with dipping

Dinner: Air Fried Empanadas

Wednesday (Day 3)

Breakfast: Asparagus Frittata

Lunch: Crispy Air Fryer Fish

Snack: Air Fryer Onion Rings with dipping

Dinner: Air Fryer Lemon Garlic Shrimp

Thursday (Day 4)

Breakfast: Mushroom Oatmeal

Lunch: Chicken Fajitas

Snack: Air Fryer Chicken Nuggets

Dinner: Sriracha & Honey Tossed Calamari

Friday (Day 5)

Breakfast: Air Fryer Egg Rolls

Lunch: Air Fryer Delicata Squash

Snack: Zucchini Parmesan Chips

Dinner: Air Fryer Crispy Fish Sandwich

Saturday (Day 6)

Breakfast: Air Fryer Salmon cakes

Lunch: Air Fryer Popcorn Chicken

Snack: Zucchini Gratin

Dinner: Air Fryer Lemon Pepper Shrimp

Sunday (Day 7)

Breakfast: Air Fryer Egg Rolls

Lunch: Air Fryer Crispy Fish Sticks

Snack: One Blueberry Muffin

Dinner: Air-Fried Buttermilk Chicken

Week 2

Monday (Day 8)

Breakfast: Air-Fried Spinach Frittata

Lunch: Crispy Air Fryer Brussels Sprouts

Snack: Slice of Vegan Cake

Dinner: Air Fryer Turkey Breast

Tuesday (Day 9)

Breakfast: Mushroom Omelet

Lunch: Coconut Shrimp

Dinner: Juicy Turkey Burgers with Zucchini

Wednesday (Day 10)

Breakfast: Mushroom Oatmeal

Lunch: Air Fryer Fish and Chips

Snack: Slice of Berry Cheesecake

Dinner: Air Fryer Meatloaf

Thursday (Day 11)

Breakfast: Lemon-Garlic Tofu

Lunch: Air Fryer Hamburger

Snack: Slice of Carrot Cake

Dinner: Air-Fried Buttermilk Chicken

Friday (Day 12)

Breakfast: Air-fryer omelet

Lunch: Air Fried Empanadas

Snack: Zucchini Chips

Dinner: Air Fry Rib-Eye Steak

Saturday (Day 13)

Breakfast: Breakfast Bombs

Lunch: Orange Chicken Wings

Snack: Low Carb Pork Dumplings with Dipping Sauce

Dinner: Air Fryer Chicken & Broccoli

Sunday (Day 14)

Breakfast: Air-fryer baked eggs

Lunch: Air Fryer Low Carb Chicken Bites

Snack: Half Sugar Free Brownie

Dinner: Air-Fried Turkey Breast with Maple Mustard Glaze

Week 3

Monday (Day 15)

Breakfast: Crisp egg cups

Lunch: Sweet potato fries

Snack: One Apple Cider Donut

Dinner: Air Fryer Whole Wheat Crusted Pork Chops

Tuesday (Day 16)

Breakfast: Vegan Breakfast Sandwich

Lunch: Air Fryer Delicata Squash

Snack: Air Fryer Kale Chips

Dinner: Air-Fried Chicken Pie

Wednesday (Day 17)

Breakfast: Vegan mashed potato bowl

Lunch: Chicken Fajitas

Snack: One blueberry muffin

Dinner: Garlic Parmesan Crusted Salmon

Thursday (Day 18)

Breakfast: Toad in the hole tarts

Lunch: Air Fryer Low Carb Chicken Bites

Snack: Avocado fries

Dinner: Air Fryer Hamburger

Friday (Day 19)

Breakfast: Breakfast bombs

Lunch: Air Fryer Chicken & Broccoli

Snack: Onion rings

Dinner: Air Fryer Sesame Seeds Fish Fillet

Saturday (Day 20)

Breakfast: Mushroom Omelet

Lunch: Garlic Parmesan Crusted Salmon

Snack: Roasted corn

Dinner: Chicken Fajitas

Sunday (Day 21)

Breakfast: Avocado Egg Rolls

Lunch: Air Fryer Lemon Pepper Shrimp

Snack: Zucchini Parmesan Chips

Dinner: Air Fry Rib-Eye Steak

Week 4

Monday (Day 22)

Breakfast: Apple fritter

Lunch: Air-Fried Rosemary Garlic Grilled Prawns

Dinner: Mustard Glazed Air Fryer Pork Tenderloin

Tuesday (Day 23)

Breakfast: Lemon-Garlic Tofu

Lunch: Air Fryer Turkey Breast Tenderloin

Snack: Small slice of sugar-free berry cheesecake

Dinner: Air Fryer Lemon Pepper Shrimp

Wednesday (Day 24)

Breakfast: Vegan Breakfast Sandwich

Lunch: Air Fryer Chicken & Broccoli

Snack: Slice of Carrot Cake

Dinner: Air-Fried Rosemary Garlic Grilled Prawns

Thursday (Day 25)

Breakfast: Egg Air-Fryer Omelet

Lunch: Air Fryer Southwest Chicken

Snack: Air-fry Brownie

Dinner: Air Fryer Sesame Seeds Fish Fillet

Friday (Day 26)

Breakfast: Slice of eggless and vegan cake

Lunch: Air Fryer Low Carb Chicken Bites

Snack: Kale chips

Dinner: Air Fryer Turkey Breast Tenderloin

Saturday (Day 27)

Breakfast: Bell Pepper Frittata

Lunch: Air-Fried Buttermilk Chicken

Snack: Chicken Nuggets

Dinner: Air Fry Rib-Eye Steak

Sunday (Day 28)

Breakfast: Air-fryer Spanakopita Bites

Lunch: Orange Chicken Wings

Snack: One peanut butter cookie

Dinner: Air Fryer Hamburger

Week 5

Monday (Day 29)

Breakfast: Toad in the hole Tart

Lunch: Crab cakes

Snack: Air Fryer Roasted Corn

Dinner: Air Fried Empanadas

Tuesday (Day 30)

Breakfast: Banana muffin with coffee

Lunch: Lemon Rosemary Chicken

Snack: Egg rolls

Dinner: Air Fryer Delicata Squash

CPSIA information can be obtained
at www.ICGtesting.com
Printed in the USA
BVHW050810030621
608731BV00009B/1535